Solo Traveler's Handbook

Safety Tips and Best Destinations for Independent Explorers

Monica Wolfe

Solo Traveler's Handbook

TABLE OF CONTENTS

Chapter 1: Planning Your Solo Adventure

Choosing the Right Destination

Choosing the right destination for your travels is a crucial step that can greatly influence the success and enjoyment of your journey. Whether you're a seasoned globetrotter or a novice explorer, selecting a destination involves a blend of personal interests, practical considerations, and a bit of research. This chapter delves into the key factors to consider when deciding where to go, ensuring your choice aligns with your expectations and travel goals.

Start by reflecting on your interests and preferences. Think about what excites you: is it the allure of urban landscapes with their bustling streets and rich cultural offerings, or do you find solace in nature's tranquility, with mountains, beaches, and forests calling your name? Perhaps you're drawn to historical sites that tell the stories of ancient civilizations, or maybe you're a foodie eager to sample the world's culinary delights. Your destination should resonate with your passions, as this connection will enhance every aspect of your trip.

Safety is another paramount consideration. Research the safety ratings of potential destinations, using resources like travel advisories from government websites and reviews from fellow travelers. Look into the political stability, crime rates, and health risks associated with each location. While no place is entirely without risk, some regions are known for being particularly safe for tourists. Countries like Japan, Iceland, and New Zealand often top the lists of safest destinations, providing peace of mind for travelers.

Language and communication can significantly impact your travel experience. If you're planning to visit a country where the language is unfamiliar, consider how comfortable you are with navigating potential language barriers. In many major cities, English is widely spoken, and you can often get by with basic phrases and a translation app. However, in more remote areas, you might encounter fewer English speakers, which could add a layer of challenge but also a sense of adventure. Preparing by learning some key phrases in the local language can go a long way in easing communication and showing respect for the local culture.

Cultural differences and customs are also essential to consider. Understanding and respecting local traditions can enrich your travel experience and help you avoid inadvertently offending your hosts. Research cultural norms and etiquette, such as appropriate dress codes, dining manners, and social behaviors. For instance, in some cultures, it's customary to remove your shoes before entering a home, while in others, tipping is not expected and can even be considered rude. Being aware of these nuances shows cultural sensitivity and enhances your interactions with locals.

Climate and weather conditions at your destination can significantly influence your travel plans. Consider the best time of year to visit based on the climate and seasonal events. Some destinations have a distinct peak tourist season when weather conditions are ideal but crowds are larger and prices higher. Visiting during the shoulder season, just before or after the peak, can offer a balance of good weather, fewer tourists, and better deals. For example, Europe in late spring or early fall provides pleasant weather and fewer crowds compared to the summer months.

Accessibility and convenience are practical factors that can affect your travel experience. Consider the ease of getting to your destination, including flight availability, visa requirements, and transportation options once you arrive. Direct flights are more convenient but often more expensive, while connecting flights can save money but add travel time and potential complications. Additionally, think about the internal infrastructure of your chosen destination. Efficient public transportation systems, well-maintained roads, and reliable services can make your trip smoother and more enjoyable.

Budget is a critical aspect of choosing a destination. Your financial resources will dictate many aspects of your trip, from the length of your stay to the types of activities you can afford. Some destinations are inherently more expensive due to the cost of living, currency exchange rates, and tourism demand. Western Europe, for instance, tends to be pricier than Southeast Asia. However, with careful planning and budgeting, you can find affordable options in almost any part of the world.

Research average costs for accommodation, food, transportation, and activities to gauge whether a destination fits within your budget.

Personal comfort and health considerations should not be overlooked. If you have specific health needs or dietary restrictions, research how well these can be accommodated at your destination. Access to medical facilities, availability of necessary medications, and the quality of healthcare are vital factors, especially if you have ongoing health concerns. Additionally, consider the physical demands of your chosen destination. Some trips, like trekking in the Himalayas or exploring ancient ruins, require a certain level of fitness and stamina.

The purpose of your trip can also guide your destination choice. Are you looking to relax and unwind, or do you seek adventure and excitement? A beach resort in the Maldives offers a vastly different experience from a safari in Kenya or a city break in New York. If you're traveling for a special occasion, such as a honeymoon or anniversary, choose a destination that adds a sense of romance and celebration. Conversely, if you're traveling for personal growth or to challenge yourself, destinations that push you out of your comfort zone might be more appropriate.

Sustainability and ethical considerations are increasingly important for many travelers. Think about the environmental and social impact of your visit. Choose destinations that promote sustainabletourism practices and support local communities. Destinations like Costa Rica and Bhutan have made significant strides in eco-friendly tourism, offering experiences that allow you to enjoy natural beauty while minimizing your ecological footprint. Research accommodations that are committed to sustainability, such as those with eco-certifications or practices like reducing plastic use and conserving water. Additionally, consider how you can contribute positively to the local economy, perhaps by staying in locally-owned lodgings, dining at local restaurants, and purchasing souvenirs directly from artisans.

Traveling without a well-thought-out itinerary can be like setting sail without a map. Crafting a realistic itinerary is an art that balances structure with flexibility, ensuring you make the most of your time while leaving room for spontaneous adventures. A good itinerary enhances your travel experience by helping you prioritize activities, manage your time efficiently, and avoid unnecessary stress. Here's how to master the process.

The first step in creating a realistic itinerary is understanding the purpose and goals of your trip. Are you seeking relaxation, adventure, cultural immersion, or perhaps a mix of all three? Your travel goals will shape your itinerary by determining the types of activities you include and the pace of your trip. For example, a relaxation-focused trip might involve fewer activities with more downtime, while an adventure-packed journey may require more detailed planning and precise time management.

Once your goals are clear, research is crucial. Start by gathering information about your destination. This includes understanding the geography, key attractions, local customs, and transportation options. Travel guides, blogs, forums, and social media groups can provide valuable insights and firsthand experiences. Pay attention to opening hours, seasonal variations, and any special events or festivals that might affect your plans. This groundwork will help you identify must-see sites, hidden gems, and potential challenges.

With this foundation, begin to outline the major components of your itinerary. Start with your arrival and departure dates, as these bookend your trip and provide the framework for your schedule. Next, allocate days or half-days to major attractions or activities. Be realistic about how much you can accomplish in a day, considering factors like travel time between locations, the physical demands of activities, and the need for rest and meals.

One effective strategy is to group activities by their proximity to each other. This minimizes travel time and maximizes your time exploring. For instance, if you're visiting Paris, you might spend one day exploring the Louvre, the Tuileries Garden, and the Musée d'Orsay, all of which are within walking distance. The next day could be dedicated to the Eiffel Tower, the Champ de Mars, and the nearby Rue Cler market. This approach not only saves time but also provides a more coherent and enjoyable experience.

Flexibility is key to a successful itinerary. While it's tempting to pack your schedule with activities, over-planning can lead to burnout and prevent you from enjoying the moment. Include buffer time between activities to account for unexpected delays, leisurely meals, or spontaneous detours. Designate one or two "free" days or afternoons where you have no fixed plans, allowing you to explore at your own pace or revisit favorite spots.

Consider the practical aspects of your itinerary. Factor in transportation logistics, such as the time it takes to travel between destinations and the best modes of transport. Public transportation, rideshares, and walking are often more efficient and immersive ways to get around in urban areas. For longer distances, research train schedules, bus routes, and flight options. Always have a Plan B for transportation, as delays and cancellations can and do happen.

Accommodation choices can also impact your itinerary. Staying in centrally located lodgings can save you time and money on transportation. Look for hotels, hostels, or vacation rentals that are close to the main attractions you plan to visit. If you're traveling to multiple cities or regions, consider the logistics of changing accommodations, and try to minimize the number of times you switch lodgings to reduce the hassle of packing and unpacking.

Meal planning is another important element. While you don't need to schedule every meal, having a general idea of where you'll eat can save time and prevent hunger-induced crankiness. Research popular local eateries, especially those that require reservations. Consider mixing sit-down meals with quicker options like street food or picnics, which can be both time-efficient and budget-friendly.

Health and well-being should not be overlooked in your itinerary. Schedule time for rest and relaxation, especially if your trip involves strenuous activities or long days of sightseeing. Ensure you stay hydrated, wear comfortable clothing and shoes, and get enough sleep. If you're crossing multiple time zones, allow for some adjustment time to combat jet lag.

Budgeting is integral to a realistic itinerary. Outline your daily expenses, including accommodations, meals, transportation, entrance fees, and souvenirs. Keep track of your spending to avoid running out of money midway through your trip. Being mindful of your budget can also help you make informed decisions about which activities and attractions are worth the splurge and where you can save.

Traveling with companions adds another layer of complexity to itinerary planning. Ensure that everyone's interests and needs are considered. This might mean compromising on certain activities or splitting up for part of the day to pursue different interests. Clear communication and flexibility are essential to maintaining harmony and ensuring everyone enjoys the trip.

Technology can be a valuable tool in planning and managing your itinerary. Use travel apps and digital calendars to organize your schedule, set reminders, and keep important information at your fingertips. Apps like Google Maps, TripIt, and local transit apps can help you navigate and adjust your plans on the go. Having digital backups of your itinerary, reservations, and important documents can also provide peace of mind in case of lost or stolen items.

Traveling solo offers unparalleled freedom, but it also requires careful financial planning to ensure you can enjoy your journey without constantly worrying about money. Budgeting for solo travel involves more than just setting aside a lump sum; it requires a detailed plan that accounts for all potential expenses, provides a cushion for unexpected costs, and aligns with your travel goals and lifestyle.

The first step in budgeting for solo travel is determining your total travel fund. This includes any savings specifically set aside for the trip, as well as potential income from selling items, freelancing, or working remotely while traveling. Be realistic about how much you can save before your departure date. If your current savings fall short of your target, consider ways to cut back on non-essential expenses or find additional sources of income. A clear understanding of your financial resources will guide your budgeting process and help you make informed decisions.

Once you have a grasp on your available funds, break down your budget into key categories: transportation, accommodation, food, activities, insurance, and miscellaneous expenses. This segmentation helps you allocate your money strategically and track your spending more effectively.

Transportation costs can vary widely depending on your destination and travel style. Start by researching flights, trains, buses, and other transportation modes. Use comparison websites to find the best deals on airfare and consider alternative airports or travel dates if your schedule is flexible. For ground transportation, look into local options such as public transit, bike rentals, or walking, which can be more economical than taxis or rideshares. If you're planning to rent a car, factor in the costs of fuel, insurance, and parking.

Accommodation is often one of the largest expenses for solo travelers, but there are ways to manage these costs. Consider a range of options, from budget hostels and guesthouses to vacation rentals and homestays. Booking platforms like Airbnb and Booking.com offer various price points and allow you to read reviews to ensure quality and safety. Additionally, look for accommodations with kitchen facilities, which can save you money on meals. For longer stays, negotiate weekly or monthly rates, which are often cheaper than nightly prices.

Food expenses can add up quickly, especially if you eat out for every meal. To keep costs down, mix dining out with grocery shopping and cooking your own meals. Street food and local markets often provide delicious, authentic meals at a fraction of the cost of restaurants. If you do dine out, prioritize lunch over dinner, as many restaurants offer lunch specials that are more affordable. Be mindful of snack and beverage costs, which can sneak up on you if you're not careful.

Activities and sightseeing are essential parts of any travel experience, but they can also strain your budget. Prioritize free or low-cost activities such as walking tours, hiking, visiting parks or public beaches, and exploring local neighborhoods. Research museums and attractions that offer free entry on certain days or discounted rates for students, seniors, or early bookings. For paid activities, read reviews and compare prices to ensure you're getting the best value for your money.

Travel insurance is a non-negotiable expense that protects you from unforeseen circumstances such as medical emergencies, trip cancellations, or lost belongings. While it might seem like an extra cost, the peace of mind it provides is invaluable. Shop around for policies that offer the coverage you need at a price you can afford. Be sure to read the fine print and understand what is and isn't covered.

Miscellaneous expenses can include anything from souvenirs and tips to laundry and internet access. These costs can be harder to predict, so allocate a portion of your budget for unexpected expenses. A good rule of thumb is to set aside at least 10-15% of your total budget for these unforeseen costs.

To keep your budget on track while traveling, use budgeting apps to monitor your spending. Apps like Trail Wallet, TravelSpend, or even a simple spreadsheet can help you log expenses and compare them against your budget. Regularly reviewing your spending allows you to make adjustments as needed and avoid running out of money.

Another important aspect of budgeting for solo travel is managing your money on the go. Carry a mix of cash and cards to ensure you have multiple payment options. Notify your bank of your travel plans to avoid any issues with card transactions abroad. Consider using a travel credit card that offers no foreign transaction fees and rewards points or cashback on purchases. Additionally, keep an eye on currency exchange rates and use ATMs wisely to minimize fees.

Safety and security are also crucial when managing your travel budget. Keep your money and valuables secure by using a money belt or hidden pouch. Avoid carrying large amounts of cash and use hotel safes where available. Be cautious of scams and always trust your instincts when dealing with money matters.

While it's important to stick to your budget, don't forget to enjoy yourself. Allow room for spontaneity and treat yourself occasionally. If you come across an unexpected opportunity or experience that's slightly over budget but worth it, don't be afraid to adjust your spending in other areas to accommodate it. The goal is to have a memorable and fulfilling trip, not to be so restrictive that you miss out on what makes travel special.

Reflecting on your spending habits both during and after the trip can provide valuable insights for future travels. Take note of areas where you overspent and consider how you can better manage these expenses next time. Conversely, if you find that you consistently under-budgeted certain categories, adjust your planning accordingly. This reflection helps improve your budgeting skills and ensures more accurate and effective financial planning for subsequent trips.

Choosing the right accommodation can significantly influence the quality of your travel experience. With myriad options available, ranging from luxurious hotels to quaint bed-and-breakfasts, the process can be overwhelming. This chapter delves into the nuances of booking accommodations, offering practical advice to ensure you find the perfect place to stay, tailored to your needs and preferences.

Start by identifying your priorities. Are you looking for comfort, affordability, or a unique experience? Understanding what matters most will help narrow your choices. For some, proximity to local attractions or public transportation is crucial, while others might prioritize amenities such as free breakfast, a pool, or a fitness center. Once you have a clear idea of your priorities, create a list of must-haves and nice-to-haves to guide your search.

The next step is to determine your budget. Accommodations can range from a few dollars a night in a hostel to several hundred in a five-star hotel. Setting a budget early on will prevent you from wasting time on options that are out of your price range. Consider all potential costs, including taxes, service fees, and any additional charges for extra amenities or services.

Online booking platforms are an invaluable resource in the accommodation search. Websites like Booking.com, Airbnb, Expedia, and Hostelworld offer extensive listings and user reviews. These platforms provide filters that allow you to sort by price, location, and amenities, making it easier to find options that meet your criteria. Pay close attention to user reviews and ratings, as they offer insight into the experiences of previous guests. Look for patterns in the reviews—if multiple people mention the same issue, it's likely a recurring problem.

When reading reviews, it's essential to consider the source. Reviews from seasoned travelers might be more discerning than those from occasional vacationers. Additionally, some reviews may be biased or influenced by personal preferences that don't align with yours. Cross-referencing reviews from multiple platforms can provide a more balanced perspective.

Once you've shortlisted potential accommodations, visit their official websites. Sometimes booking directly through a hotel or property's site can yield better deals or additional perks, such as free breakfast or late checkout. Moreover, direct bookings often come with flexible cancellation policies, which can be a significant advantage if your plans change.

Location is a critical factor. A hotel in the heart of the city might be convenient for sightseeing but could be noisy and more expensive. On the other hand, accommodations further from the center might offer a more peaceful stay and better value for money. Use maps to check the distance from key attractions, public transportation, and essential services like grocery stores and restaurants. Google Maps and other mapping services often provide a street view, allowing you to get a sense of the neighborhood.

Consider the type of accommodation that best suits your travel style. Hotels offer a range of services and amenities, including daily housekeeping, room service, and concierge assistance. They are ideal for travelers seeking convenience and a higher level of service. Bed-and-breakfasts provide a more personal touch, often run by local hosts who can offer insider tips about the area. Hostels are a budget-friendly option, particularly for solo travelers or those looking to meet fellow adventurers. They typically offer shared dormitory-style rooms, though many also have private rooms available.

Vacation rentals, such as those found on Airbnb or Vrbo, offer the comfort of a home away from home. They are perfect for families, groups, or anyone planning an extended stay. These properties often come with kitchens, allowing you to save money by preparing your own meals. However, they may lack the on-site services provided by hotels.

For those seeking unique experiences, consider alternative accommodations. Boutique hotels, eco-lodges, and even treehouses or yurts can offer memorable stays that go beyond the typical hotel room. These options often reflect the local culture and environment, providing a more immersive travel experience.

Negotiating the best deal is an art worth mastering. Start by comparing prices across different platforms to ensure you're getting a competitive rate. If you find a lower price on a third-party site, contact the accommodation directly to see if they can match or beat the offer. Many hotels are willing to negotiate, especially if you're booking for an extended stay or during a low season.

Timing your booking can also affect the price. Generally, booking well in advance secures the best rates, particularly for popular destinations or peak travel seasons. However, if you're flexible with your travel dates, last-minute deals can sometimes offer significant savings. Keep an eye on price trends and set up alerts on booking platforms to be notified of price drops.

Loyalty programs and memberships can also provide valuable savings. Many hotel chains have loyalty programs that offer discounts, free nights, and other perks to frequent guests. Additionally, memberships in organizations like AAA or AARP often come with accommodation discounts. If you travel frequently, it's worth signing up for these programs to take advantage of the benefits.

Before finalizing your booking, review the cancellation policy carefully. Flexible cancellation policies provide peace of mind, allowing you to change your plans without incurring hefty fees. However, thesepolicies often come with a slightly higher price tag. If your travel dates are set in stone, a non-refundable rate might save you money. Always weigh the risks and benefits based on your specific situation.

Transportation: Planes, Trains, and Automobiles

Traveling from one place to another is one of the most critical aspects of any journey. Whether you're planning a weekend getaway or an extended vacation, understanding the various transportation options available can make a significant difference in your overall experience. This chapter provides practical advice on navigating the world of planes, trains, and automobiles, ensuring you make informed decisions that suit your travel style, budget, and preferences.

When it comes to air travel, the first step is to search for flights well in advance. Airlines often release tickets up to a year before the departure date, and booking early can help you secure the best prices. Use flight comparison websites like Skyscanner, Google Flights, or Kayak to compare fares across different airlines and booking platforms. Flexible dates can also lead to better deals, so if your schedule allows, consider adjusting your travel dates by a few days to find lower prices.

Loyalty programs and frequent flyer miles can provide significant savings for regular travelers. Signing up for an airline's loyalty program is free and can offer benefits such as priority boarding, free checked bags, and access to airport lounges. Additionally, credit cards that offer travel rewards can help you accumulate points or miles that can be redeemed for future flights, hotel stays, or even car rentals.

When booking a flight, carefully review the airline's baggage policy. Low-cost carriers often have strict baggage allowances and hefty fees for exceeding them. Pack strategically to avoid these charges, and consider investing in a lightweight, durable suitcase that complies with carry-on size restrictions. For long-haul flights, comfort is key. Bring a neck pillow, noise-canceling headphones, and a good book or downloaded movies to make the journey more enjoyable.

Trains offer a different kind of travel experience, often providing scenic routes and a more relaxed pace. In many regions, trains are a convenient and affordable way to explore multiple destinations. For instance, Europe boasts an extensive rail network, making it easy to travel between cities and countries. Rail passes, such as the Eurail Pass, offer flexible travel options and can be cost-effective for those planning to make several stops.

Booking train tickets in advance can also yield significant savings, especially for high-speed trains and popular routes. Websites like Trainline, Rail Europe, and national railway operators' sites allow you to compare schedules and prices. Be sure to check if there are any discounts available for students, seniors, or groups.

Traveling by train can be a social experience as well. Many trains have dining cars or lounges where you can meet fellow travelers. Overnight trains, with sleeper cabins, offer the added convenience of combining travel and accommodation, saving both time and money. Pack snacks and entertainment for the journey, as not all trains offer food service, and having a book, music, or games can make the trip more enjoyable.

Automobiles provide the greatest flexibility and independence, allowing you to explore destinations off the beaten path. Renting a car is often the best option for rural areas or regions with limited public transportation. When choosing a rental car, consider the size and type of vehicle that best suits your needs. A compact car might be more economical and easier to park in cities, while a larger vehicle or SUV might be necessary for carrying luggage or navigating rough terrain.

Before booking a rental car, compare prices on websites like Rentalcars.com, Expedia, and the rental companies' direct sites. Look for discounts or promotional codes that can reduce the cost. Pay attention to the rental agreement's terms, including mileage limits, fuel policies, and insurance coverage. While rental companies offer their own insurance, you may already be covered through your personal auto insurance or credit card benefits.

Driving in a foreign country can be a unique challenge. Familiarize yourself with local traffic laws, road signs, and driving customs before you go. In some countries, an International Driving Permit (IDP) is required, so check if you need one and how to obtain it. GPS navigation systems or smartphone apps like Google Maps and Waze are invaluable tools for finding your way, but it's also wise to have a physical map as a backup.

Road trips are a fantastic way to see a country at your own pace. Plan your route ahead of time, but leave room for spontaneity. Some of the best travel experiences come from unexpected detours and stops. Pack an emergency kit with essentials like a first aid kit, flashlight, and basic tools. Snacks, water, and a playlist of your favorite music or podcasts can make long drives more enjoyable.

Combining different modes of transportation can often enhance your travel experience. For example, you might fly into a major city, take a train to a nearby region, and then rent a car to explore the countryside. This approach allows you to take advantage of the strengths of each mode of transport—speed and convenience of flights, scenic and relaxed pace of trains, and the freedom and flexibility of cars.

When planning your transportation, consider the environmental impact of your choices. Air travel has the highest carbon footprint per mile, so look for direct flights to reduce emissions. Trains are generally more eco-friendly, and many rail companies are investingin green technologies to further minimize their impact. When renting a car, consider opting for a hybrid or electric vehicle if available. Additionally, carpooling or sharing rides with other travelers can reduce the number of vehicles on the road and lower your overall carbon footprint.

What to Pack: The Basics

Packing for a journey, whether it's a short weekend getaway or an extended adventure, requires thoughtful consideration to ensure you have everything you need without overburdening yourself. The essentials you pack can make or break your travel experience, and understanding what is truly necessary can help streamline the process.

First, selecting the right luggage is paramount. Your choice of bag should reflect the nature of your trip. A carry-on suitcase is ideal for most trips, offering mobility and avoiding the hassle and fees associated with checked bags. Opt for a suitcase with sturdy wheels and a comfortable handle, as ease of transport is crucial. For more adventurous or longer trips, a durable backpack might be more suitable. Look for one with multiple compartments to help keep your belongings organized and easily accessible.

When it comes to clothing, versatility is key. Choose items that can be mixed and matched to create various outfits. Neutral colors and simple patterns work best as they can be easily paired with different items. Focus on packing lightweight, quick-dry fabrics. These materials are not only comfortable but also easy to wash and dry, making them perfect for travel. Depending on the destination and the length of your trip, plan to pack enough clothing for about a week and do laundry as needed. This strategy keeps your luggage light and manageable.

Footwear should be chosen based on the activities you plan to engage in. Comfortable walking shoes are a must, as traveling often involves a lot of exploration on foot. If you're heading to a region with rugged terrain or planning on hiking, pack a pair of durable, supportive hiking boots. Additionally, a pair of versatile sandals or flip-flops can be useful for casual outings or if you're staying in accommodations with shared showers.

Toiletries are another critical component of your packing list. Transfer liquids such as shampoo, conditioner, and body wash into travel-sized containers to save space. Solid toiletries, like bar soap and shampoo bars, can also be a great way to reduce bulk. Don't forget to pack a toothbrush, toothpaste, deodorant, and any prescription medications you may need. A small first aid kit with band-aids, antiseptic wipes, pain relievers, and any personal health items can be invaluable for minor emergencies.

Electronics have become indispensable for modern travel. A smartphone is likely your most versatile tool, serving as a camera, map, communication device, and entertainment center. Ensure you have a reliable charger and consider bringing a portable battery pack in case you're away from power sources for extended periods. If you're bringing other electronics like a tablet, e-reader, or laptop, make sure they're necessary for your trip to avoid unnecessary weight. Additionally, a universal plug adapter is essential if you're traveling internationally to accommodate different electrical outlets.

Security is particularly important when traveling. Consider investing in anti-theft bags or accessories with features like lockable zippers and RFID-blocking pockets to protect against electronic pickpocketing. A money belt or hidden pouch can keep your important documents and cash safe. Make copies of your passport, travel insurance, and other critical documents, storing them separately from the originals. Digital copies stored in a secure cloud service can also provide a backup in case of loss.

Entertainment and comfort items can significantly enhance your travel experience. Bring a good book, travel journal, or download some movies or TV shows onto your device for downtime. A reusable water bottle is not only environmentally friendly but also keeps you hydrated, which is essential for your well-being. An eye mask and earplugs or noise-canceling headphones can help you sleep better on planes, trains, or in noisy accommodations, ensuring you stay rested and ready for your adventures.

Packing cubes are a traveler's best friend, helping to keep your bag organized and making it easier to find items without unpacking everything. They come in various sizes and can be used to separate clothing, toiletries, and other items. Compression bags can also be useful for reducing the volume of your clothes, leaving more room for other essentials.

Consider the specifics of your destination and activities when packing. For example, if you're heading to a beach destination, pack a swimsuit, sunscreen, and a quick-dry towel. For colder climates, ensure you have a warm coat, gloves, and a hat. Researching your destination beforehand can help you pack appropriately and avoid bringing unnecessary items.

A travel guidebook or notes on your destination can be incredibly helpful, especially when you're navigating new cities or looking for recommendations. Offline maps and language translation apps can also be lifesavers when you don't have internet access.

Solo travel can be unpredictable, so it's good to be prepared for various scenarios. A lightweight rain jacket or poncho can protect you from unexpected showers. A small sewing kit can fix minor clothing mishaps. Multi-purpose tools, like a Swiss Army knife, can come in handy in numerous situations, though be sure to pack them in your checked luggage if flying.

Finally, consider your personal comfort and needs. Solo travel allows for complete independence, so pack items that will make you feel secure and comfortable. Whether it's a favorite snack, a small piece of homelike a cherished photo, or a travel-sized comfort item like a cozy scarf or blanket, these little touches can make a big difference in your overall travel experience.

Tech Gear and Gadgets

Packing the right tech gear and gadgets can greatly enhance your travel experience. Whether you're a digital nomad, a casual traveler, or an adventurer heading off the beaten path, the right tools can provide convenience, safety, and entertainment. However, striking the right balance between necessity and excess is crucial to avoid overloading your luggage and complicating your trip.

First and foremost, a smartphone is indispensable. It serves multiple purposes, acting as your camera, GPS, communication device, and entertainment center. Beyond the basics, consider the apps that can make your travels smoother. Download offline maps for navigation in areas with spotty internet, and translation apps for overcoming language barriers. Travel-specific apps like currency converters, weather forecasts, and public transportation guides can also be incredibly useful. Ensure your phone is unlocked, allowing you to use local SIM cards to save on roaming charges.

A reliable power bank is a must-have, especially when you're on the go and away from reliable power sources. Look for a high-capacity model that can charge your smartphone multiple times. Some power banks come with additional features like built-in cables, fast charging capabilities, or solar panels, which can be handy if you're traveling to remote areas.

For those who rely heavily on their laptops for work or leisure, choosing the right one is key. Lightweight, durable models with long battery life are ideal for travel. Consider the types of ports available and bring the necessary adapters, especially if you use peripherals like external hard drives or projectors. A good laptop sleeve or case will protect your device from the bumps and jolts of travel. Additionally, a privacy screen can be useful in public places, keeping your work private without hindering your productivity.

Tablets can be a great alternative or complement to laptops, providing similar functionality with less bulk. They are perfect for reading, watching movies, or even sketching if you're creatively inclined. Accessories like a detachable keyboard or a stylus can enhance their usability. E-readers are another excellent option for avid readers, offering a lightweight way to carry your entire library. Choose a model with a backlight for reading in low-light conditions and a long battery life for extended periods without charging.

Photography enthusiasts will want to pack a good camera, though the decision between a DSLR, mirrorless, or compact camera depends on your priorities. DSLRs and mirrorless cameras offer superior image quality and flexibility with interchangeable lenses, but they can be bulky and heavy. Compact cameras, on the other hand, are more portable and still provide decent image quality. Don't forget spare batteries, memory cards, and a sturdy camera bag. A small tripod or a

Gorillapod can be useful for stable shots, especially in low-light conditions or for long exposures.

Audio equipment is another consideration. Good quality headphones can be a traveler's best friend, providing entertainment and drowning out background noise. Noise-canceling headphones are particularly valuable on planes and in busy public spaces. If you need to make conference calls or record audio, a small external microphone can significantly improve sound quality. Compact Bluetooth speakers are great for sharing music or podcasts in your accommodation without relying on potentially subpar hotel room setups.

Staying connected while traveling can be challenging, but a portable Wi-Fi hotspot can make a big difference. These devices allow you to connect multiple devices to a single internet source, often providing better speeds and reliability than local Wi-Fi networks. Researching the best options for your destination and purchasing a local SIM card can save you money and provide more consistent access.

Safety should always be a priority, and tech gadgets can play a crucial role here. GPS trackers can be attached to your luggage, ensuring you can locate it if it gets lost. Personal safety apps on your smartphone can alert trusted contacts if you find yourself in a dangerous situation. Additionally, consider carrying a small, portable safe for securing valuables in your accommodation.

Traveling often involves long hours in transit, and having the right entertainment options can make these periods more enjoyable. Pre-download movies, TV shows, music, and audiobooks to your devices to avoid relying on in-flight entertainment or uncertain internet connections. Streaming services often allow offline downloads, so take advantage of these features before you leave.

For the more adventurous traveler, tech gear like action cameras can capture your exploits in stunning detail. These cameras are typically rugged, waterproof, and capable of recording high-quality video. Drones are another exciting option for capturing unique perspectives, though it's important to research local regulations and obtain necessary permits to avoid legal issues.

When packing tech gear, organization is key. Cable organizers can keep your chargers, adapters, and other small gadgets neatly arranged and easily accessible. A tech pouch or bag can store all your electronic accessories in one place, reducing the chances of losing something important. Labeling your cables and devices can also help you stay organized, especially if you're carrying multiple similar items.

Lastly, consider the environmental impact of your tech gear. Rechargeable batteries are a more sustainable option compared to disposable ones. Look for energy-efficient devices and those with eco-friendly certifications. Some companies even offer trade-in programs for old electronics, which can be agreat way to responsibly dispose of outdated tech while potentially receiving a discount on new purchases.

Health and Safety Items

Traveling opens up a world of adventure and new experiences, but ensuring your health and safety is paramount. Being prepared with the right health and safety items can make a substantial difference in how smoothly your journey unfolds. This chapter delves into the essential items you should consider packing to stay healthy and secure while on the road.

A well-stocked first aid kit is a fundamental component of your travel gear. Tailor your kit to include bandages, antiseptic wipes, adhesive tape, sterile gauze pads, and a pair of tweezers. These basics can handle minor injuries like cuts, scrapes, and splinters. Additionally, non-prescription medications such as pain relievers, antihistamines, anti-diarrheal medicine, and motion sickness tablets should be included to manage common ailments. If you're traveling to a destination where mosquito-borne diseases are prevalent, pack insect repellent with a high concentration of DEET or a natural alternative like oil of lemon eucalyptus.

Prescription medications are another critical aspect of your health preparedness. Ensure you have enough medication to last the entire trip, plus a few extra days' worth in case of delays. Keep medications in their original containers, along with a copy of your prescriptions and a letter from your doctor explaining your need for the medication. This documentation can be crucial when crossing borders or dealing with customs officials. For travelers with chronic conditions, wearing a medical alert bracelet can provide critical information to healthcare providers in case of an emergency.

Vaccinations are a proactive step in safeguarding your health. Research the recommended and required vaccines for your destination well in advance of your departure. Some vaccinations need to be administered weeks or even months before travel to be effective. Common travel vaccines include those for hepatitis A and B, typhoid, yellow fever, and rabies. The Centers for Disease Control and Prevention (CDC) and the World Health Organization (WHO) offer up-to-date information on vaccine recommendations for various destinations.

Hydration is vital, especially when traveling to hot or high-altitude locations. Carry a durable, reusable water bottle to ensure you always have access to clean drinking water. In areas where tap water isn't safe to drink, water purification tablets or a portable water filter can prevent waterborne illnesses. Staying hydrated helps maintain energy levels, supports overall health, and can prevent heat exhaustion or altitude sickness.

Hand hygiene is another crucial element of staying healthy while traveling. Carry a small bottle of hand sanitizer with at least 60% alcohol content to use when soap and water aren't available. Wet wipes can also be useful for cleaning hands and surfaces, especially in areas where sanitation standards are not up to par. These simple measures can significantly reduce your risk of gastrointestinal infections and other illnesses.

For those traveling to regions with extreme weather conditions, appropriate clothing and gear are essential. In hot climates, lightweight, breathable clothing that covers the skin can protect against sunburn and insect bites. A wide-brimmed hat and sunglasses with UV protection are also important. In colder climates, layering is key to maintaining body heat. Thermal underwear, insulated jackets, and waterproof outer layers can prevent hypothermia and frostbite. Don't forget accessories like gloves, scarves, and thermal socks.

Sun protection is critical regardless of your destination. Pack a broad-spectrum sunscreen with an SPF of at least 30, and apply it generously to all exposed skin. Reapply every two hours, or more often if you're swimming or sweating. Lip balm with SPF can protect your lips from sun damage, and after-sun lotion can soothe skin if you do get sunburned.

Travel insurance is an often-overlooked but essential component of your health and safety preparations. Comprehensive travel insurance can cover unexpected medical expenses, emergency evacuations, and trip cancellations. Be sure to read the policy details carefully to understand what is covered and any exclusions that may apply. Some policies also offer 24/7 assistance services, which can be invaluable in a crisis.

Personal safety should also be a priority. Investing in a few discreet security items can provide peace of mind. A money belt or hidden pouch can keep your valuables secure and out of sight. A doorstop alarm or portable lock can enhance security in your accommodation. A whistle or personal alarm can deter would-be attackers and draw attention in an emergency.

For travelers who enjoy outdoor activities, specific gear can enhance both safety and enjoyment. A compact, lightweight headlamp or flashlight is indispensable for nighttime navigation or emergencies. A multi-tool can be useful for a variety of tasks, from opening cans to repairing gear. If you're venturing into remote areas, a personal locator beacon (PLB) or satellite messenger can be a lifesaver, allowing you to call for help even when you're out of cellphone range.

Traveling can sometimes lead to unexpected health issues, so knowing where to seek medical care is crucial. Research the healthcare facilities available at your destination before you depart. Many countries have English-speaking doctors and internationally accredited hospitals, and knowing their locations can save valuable time in an emergency. Some travel insurance policies include access to a network of preferred providers, which can streamline the process of finding medical care.In addition to knowing the locations of healthcare facilities, familiarize yourself with the local emergency numbers and procedures. Different countries have different numbers for police, fire, and medical emergencies, so having these numbers readily available can be crucial. Store them in your phone and write them down in a travel journal or notebook for quick access.

Packing light is an art that every traveler should master. It not only makes your journey more comfortable but also reduces the stress associated with lugging around heavy bags. The key to packing light is to be strategic and deliberate about what you bring, ensuring that every item serves a purpose and ideally, multiple purposes.

One of the most effective strategies for packing light is to choose versatile clothing. Opt for neutral colors and simple styles that can be easily mixed and matched to create different outfits. A pair of dark jeans, for example, can be dressed up or down depending on the occasion. Lightweight, wrinkle-resistant fabrics are ideal because they take up less space and can be worn straight out of the suitcase. Consider packing items that can be layered, which is particularly useful for varying climates. A lightweight sweater or cardigan can add warmth on cool evenings and can be easily removed when the temperature rises.

Footwear is often one of the bulkiest items in your luggage, so choose wisely. Ideally, limit yourself to two pairs: a comfortable pair for walking and a slightly dressier option for evenings out. Depending on your destination, a pair of versatile sandals or lightweight sneakers can work well for both casual and semiformal settings. Wear your bulkiest shoes during travel to save space in your luggage.

Toiletries can also take up a significant amount of space, but there are ways to minimize their impact. Transfer liquids and creams into small, travel-sized containers. Many drugstores sell empty bottles specifically designed for this purpose. Solid toiletries, such as bar soap, shampoo bars, and solid lotion sticks, are another excellent way to save space and avoid the hassle of liquid restrictions at airports. Remember that many hotels and accommodations provide basic toiletries, so you may not need to bring as much as you think.

When it comes to electronics, be selective. A smartphone can serve multiple functions, including as a camera, GPS, and entertainment device. If you need to bring a laptop or tablet, choose lightweight models and consider digitalizing as much as possible to avoid carrying bulky books and papers. A portable charger is essential to keep your devices powered up on the go. Don't forget to pack the necessary chargers and adapters, but try to limit the number of gadgets you bring to the bare essentials.

Rolling your clothes instead of folding them can save a surprising amount of space and reduce wrinkles. Compression bags are another great tool for maximizing space, particularly for bulkier items like jackets and sweaters. Packing cubes can help keep your belongings organized and make it easier to find what you need without unpacking everything.

A well-organized carry-on bag can also enhance your travel experience. Pack items that you'll need during the flight or immediately upon arrival, such as a change of clothes, essential toiletries, medications, and important documents. Keep your valuables, such as your passport, money, and electronics, in your carry-on to ensure they are always within reach. When packing your carry-on, consider the weight and size restrictions of your airline to avoid any issues at the gate.

One of the most challenging aspects of packing light is dealing with souvenirs and other items you acquire during your trip. To manage this, leave some extra space in your luggage when packing, or bring a lightweight, foldable bag that can be used to carry additional items on the way home. Another strategy is to mail souvenirs back home, which can often be cheaper and more convenient than trying to fit them into your suitcase.

A minimalist approach to accessories can also help lighten your load. Choose a few key pieces of jewelry that can complement multiple outfits. A lightweight scarf can serve multiple functions: as a fashion accessory, a head covering, or even a makeshift blanket on chilly flights. Sunglasses and a hat are essential for sunny destinations, but choose compact, easily packable options.

Planning your wardrobe around a specific color scheme can simplify packing and ensure that all your clothing items work together. This not only makes it easier to mix and match but also reduces the number of shoes and accessories you need to bring. Stick to a palette of two or three complementary colors, with a few accent pieces to add variety.

Laundry facilities are available in many hotels and hostels, and taking advantage of these can significantly reduce the amount of clothing you need to pack. If you're staying in one place for an extended period, consider doing laundry midway through your trip. For shorter trips, sink-washable clothing made of quick-drying fabrics can be a lifesaver. Packing a small amount of laundry detergent or laundry sheets can make this process easier.

Finally, consider the psychological benefits of packing light. Traveling with less baggage allows for greater mobility and flexibility, making it easier to navigate public transportation, walk longer distances, and adapt to unexpected changes in your itinerary. It also reduces the physical strain of carrying heavy bags and the anxiety of keeping track of numerous items.

One personal anecdote illustrates the benefits of packing light. On a trip to Europe, I initially struggled with an overstuffed suitcase and a heavy carry-on. Navigating crowded train stations and narrow hotel staircases was a nightmare. Halfway through the trip, I decided to ship a portion of my belongings back home and repacked with only the essentials. The difference was remarkable. I felt freer, more agile, and able to enjoy my journey without the constant burden of excess luggage. This experience reinforced the value of a minimalist approach to travel.

Organizing Your Backpack or Suitcase

Organizing your backpack or suitcase efficiently can transform your travel experience, making it smoother and more enjoyable. The key to effective packing lies in planning, prioritizing, and using space wisely to ensure that everything you need is easily accessible without having to rummage through your entire bag.

Start by laying out all the items you plan to bring. This allows you to see everything at once and helps you identify what's essential and what can be left behind. Group similar items together: clothes in one pile, toiletries in another, and so on. This initial step can prevent overpacking and ensure that you have a clear understanding of what you're bringing.

When it comes to clothing, consider the rule of three: three tops, three bottoms, and three pairs of underwear. This can generally suffice for a week-long trip if you mix and match. Choose versatile pieces that can be layered and accessorized differently to create multiple outfits. Roll your clothes instead of folding them. This not only saves space but also minimizes wrinkles. Place heavier items at the bottom of your suitcase or against the part of the backpack that will be closest to your back. This helps balance the weight and makes carrying the bag more comfortable.

Toiletries are another critical area to manage efficiently. Invest in travel-sized containers and fill them with your favorite products. Many stores sell small, reusable bottles that you can fill with shampoo, conditioner, and lotion. Consider solid alternatives to liquid toiletries to save space and avoid the hassle of liquid restrictions at airports. For instance, solid shampoo bars and toothpaste tablets are becoming increasingly popular among travelers.

Electronics can quickly become a tangled mess if not organized properly. Use a small pouch or bag to keep all your cords, chargers, and adapters together. Label each cord with a twist tie or a piece of tape to quickly identify which device it belongs to. If you're traveling internationally, make sure to bring the appropriate power adapters for your destination. A universal adapter is a worthwhile investment if you travel frequently.

Packing cubes are a game-changer for organizing your suitcase or backpack. These small, lightweight fabric containers help compartmentalize your belongings, making it easy to find items quickly without unpacking everything. For example, you can have one cube for tops, another for bottoms, and another for underwear and socks. Packing cubes also help compress your clothes, allowing you to fit more into your bag.

Another useful tool is a laundry bag. Designate a small, lightweight bag for dirty clothes, which keeps them separate from your clean items. This not only helps with organization but also makes it easier when you need to do laundry during your trip. Some travelers prefer to use a compression sack for dirty laundry to minimize the space it takes up.

Consider the accessibility of items you'll need frequently. Place these in an easily reachable part of your bag. For example, keep your passport, travel documents, and any necessary medications in a front pocket or the top compartment of your backpack. This way, you can quickly grab them without digging through your entire bag. It's also a good idea to have a small daypack or a foldable tote bag that you can use for day trips or carrying items you purchase along the way.

Shoes can be bulky and awkward to pack. Limit yourself to two pairs: one comfortable pair for walking and another pair for more formal occasions, if necessary. Stuff socks, underwear, or other small items inside your shoes to utilize the empty space. Place your shoes in a plastic bag or a dedicated shoe bag to keep them from dirtying your clothes. Arrange them along the edges of your suitcase or at the bottom of your backpack to help balance the weight.

When packing, think about the order in which you'll need items. Place items you won't need until you reach your destination, like evening wear or extra shoes, at the bottom of your bag. Items you'll need en route, like a sweater, book, or snacks, should be easily accessible. If you're using a backpack, consider packing in layers, with the heaviest items closest to your back for better weight distribution.

Documents and valuables should always be kept secure and within reach. Use a travel wallet or a document organizer to keep your passport, boarding passes, and important papers in one place. For added security, consider a money belt or a neck pouch that can be worn under your clothes. This is particularly useful in crowded places where pickpocketing might be a concern.

For longer trips, especially those involving multiple destinations, consider a modular packing approach. Pack smaller bags within your main suitcase or backpack, each containing items for different parts of your trip. For example, one smaller bag could hold everything you need for the first leg of your journey, while another could contain items for the second leg. This way, you only need to unpack what's necessary at each stop, keeping the rest organized and intact.

One personal experience that highlights the importance of organization involved a month-long backpacking trip through Southeast Asia. By using packing cubes and a strict packing list, I was able to fit everything I needed into a single carry-on-sized backpack.This approach made navigating airports, buses, and hostels much easier. I always knew exactly where my items were, and I could quickly grab what I needed without disrupting the rest of my belongings. The packing cubes helped keep my clothes clean and organized, and having a designated place for each type of item reduced the time spent searching for things.

Chapter 3: Safety Tips for Solo Travelers

Staying Safe in Different Environments

Traveling introduces you to a variety of environments, each with unique challenges and opportunities. Understanding how to stay safe in these different settings is crucial for a successful and enjoyable journey. From bustling urban centers to quiet rural areas, coastal regions, and wilderness adventures, every environment demands specific safety considerations.

Cities can be both thrilling and overwhelming. The constant activity, diverse population, and myriad of attractions make urban areas a favorite among travelers. However, they also pose risks such as petty theft, scams, and traffic hazards. One fundamental rule for city safety is to blend in. Dress like a local to avoid drawing unnecessary attention. Research the neighborhoods you'll be visiting to understand which areas are safe and which to avoid, especially after dark.

Public transportation is a lifeline in most cities but can also be a hotspot for pickpockets. Stay alert and keep your belongings secure. Avoid using your phone or other valuables openly on crowded public transport. Instead, carry a book or magazine to keep yourself occupied. If you need to check directions, step into a shop or a less crowded area. Late at night, it's safer to use ride-sharing services or licensed taxis rather than public transport.

Walking in cities can be a delightful way to explore, but always be aware of your surroundings. Stick to well-lit and busy streets, particularly at night. Sidewalks can be crowded, so keep your bag close and in front of you. If you feel uneasy or sense someone is following you, step into a shop or public place. Trust your instincts and never hesitate to seek help from local authorities or shopkeepers.

Rural areas, while often serene and picturesque, come with their own set of challenges. The slower pace and smaller populations can be a refreshing change from city life, but they also mean fewer resources in case of an emergency. Always inform someone of your travel plans and expected return time. In remote areas, mobile phone coverage might be spotty, so carrying a paper map and a compass can be invaluable.

When traveling in rural regions, be prepared for limited medical facilities. Carry a well-stocked first aid kit and any necessary medications. Learn basic first aid skills to handle minor injuries or illnesses. Familiarize yourself with the local flora and fauna, as some plants and animals can be dangerous. For example, knowing how to identify poisonous plants or venomous snakes can prevent accidents.

Interacting with locals in rural areas can be incredibly rewarding, offering insights into traditional ways of life. However, language barriers can be more pronounced than in urban settings. Learning a few key phrases in the local language can go a long way in building rapport and ensuring you can ask for help if needed. Respect local customs and traditions, as rural communities often hold these practices in high regard.

Coastal regions are popular for their beauty and recreational activities, but they also present unique safety concerns. One of the primary hazards is water safety. Whether you're swimming, surfing, or simply enjoying the beach, always be aware of the ocean conditions. Strong currents, rip tides, and sudden changes in weather can transform a pleasant day at the beach into a dangerous situation. Swim in designated areas supervised by lifeguards and heed warning flags and signs.

Sun exposure is another concern in coastal areas. Protect yourself by applying a high-SPF sunscreen, wearing a hat, and using sunglasses. Stay hydrated, especially during the hottest parts of the day. Dehydration and heatstroke are common issues in sunny, beachside locations. Drink plenty of water and take breaks in the shade to cool down.

If you're engaging in water sports, ensure you have the appropriate safety gear and training. For activities like snorkeling or diving, use equipment from reputable providers and follow all safety instructions. Inform someone of your plans and your expected return time. In case of an accident, knowing basic water rescue techniques can be life-saving.

Wilderness adventures, whether hiking, camping, or exploring national parks, require thorough preparation. The beauty and solitude of nature come with risks such as getting lost, encountering wildlife, or facing sudden weather changes. Before heading out, research the area extensively. Know the trails, weather patterns, and potential hazards. Carry a detailed map, a GPS device, and a fully charged phone with an extra battery or portable charger.

Equip yourself with the right gear for your wilderness adventure. This includes sturdy footwear, appropriate clothing, and sufficient food and water. A multi-tool, a flashlight, and a first aid kit should be part of your essential gear. If you're camping, ensure your tent and sleeping bag are suitable for the weather conditions. Practice setting up your camp in your backyard to become familiar with your equipment.

Wildlife encounters can be one of the most thrilling aspects of wilderness travel, but they require caution. Learn about the local wildlife and how to avoid dangerous interactions. For example, in bear country, store food in bear-proof containers and cook away from your sleeping area. If you encounter a large animal, remain calm and slowly back away. Never feed wild animals, as this can create dangerous situations for both you and the animals.

Staying aware of weather conditions is critical inthe wilderness. Weather can change rapidly, and being unprepared can lead to severe consequences such as hypothermia or heat exhaustion. Always check the weather forecast before setting out and be prepared for unexpected shifts. Layer your clothing to adjust to temperature changes and carry rain gear even if the forecast predicts clear skies. In mountainous regions, be especially cautious of altitude sickness. Ascend gradually, stay hydrated, and recognize the signs such as dizziness, headaches, and nausea.

Arriving in an unfamiliar city can be both exhilarating and daunting. The hustle and bustle, the unfamiliar streets, and the diverse array of people and cultures create a unique atmosphere that can be both captivating and overwhelming. To navigate a new city successfully, preparation, awareness, and adaptability are key.

Before setting foot in an unfamiliar city, research is essential. Understanding the layout of the city, its neighborhoods, and its public transportation system can significantly ease the initial sense of disorientation. Start by studying maps and transit routes online. Familiarize yourself with major landmarks, which can serve as reference points when you're out exploring. Many cities offer apps that provide real-time information about public transportation, including routes, schedules, and delays. Downloading these apps can save you time and reduce stress.

One of the first things to do upon arrival is to get a local SIM card or ensure you have a reliable data plan. Having access to the internet allows you to use GPS for navigation, look up information on the go, and stay connected with others. It's also wise to carry a physical map as a backup, in case your phone battery dies or you encounter areas with poor signal.

Understanding the local culture and customs can help you blend in and avoid unwanted attention. Learn a few basic phrases in the local language, such as greetings, thank you, and asking for help. Even if you're not fluent, making an effort to communicate in the local language is often appreciated and can lead to more positive interactions. Dress appropriately for the culture and the climate to further reduce the chances of standing out as a tourist.

Safety should always be a top priority when navigating unfamiliar cities. Keep your belongings secure and be mindful of your surroundings. Use a crossbody bag with zippers and keep it close to your body. Avoid carrying large amounts of cash; instead, use credit or debit cards where possible. Be wary of overly friendly strangers who might distract you while an accomplice attempts to pickpocket you. Trust your instincts—if something feels off, it probably is.

Public transportation is an efficient way to get around most cities, but it requires a bit of savvy to use effectively. In many places, buses, trams, and subways are the primary modes of transport. Learn how to read the transit maps and schedules. During rush hours, public transportation can be crowded and hectic. Keep your belongings close and be aware of pickpockets. If you're unsure of where to get off, don't hesitate to ask the driver or a fellow passenger for help.

Walking is another excellent way to explore a city and discover its hidden gems. Wear comfortable shoes and plan your routes in advance. Stick to well-lit and busy streets, especially at night. If you get lost, stay calm and use your map or GPS to find your way. Ducking into a café or shop can also provide a moment to regroup and ask for directions if needed.

Biking can be a fun and efficient way to see more of a city in a short amount of time. Many cities have bike-sharing programs that allow you to rent a bike for a few hours or a day. Make sure to familiarize yourself with local biking laws and routes. Always wear a helmet and use bike lanes where available. Lock your bike securely when not in use to prevent theft.

When it comes to dining, exploring local food markets and street vendors can be a highlight of your trip. However, it's important to ensure the food is safe to eat. Look for stalls that are busy with locals, as high turnover usually means the food is fresh. Avoid raw or undercooked items and always wash your hands or use hand sanitizer before eating.

Navigating unfamiliar cities also involves understanding the local etiquette. In some cultures, tipping is expected, while in others it may be considered rude. Learn about these practices beforehand to avoid awkward situations. Similarly, be aware of local norms regarding personal space, gestures, and behavior in public places.

Engaging with locals can greatly enhance your experience and provide valuable insights into the city's culture and history. Don't be afraid to ask for recommendations on places to visit, eat, or shop. Locals often know the best spots that aren't listed in travel guides. Joining a guided tour can also be a great way to get oriented and learn more about the city's background.

Technology can be a helpful companion in navigating a new city. Use apps for navigation, translation, and finding local attractions. Social media platforms and travel blogs can offer real-time tips and recommendations. Consider using ride-sharing apps for longer distances or when public transportation is not convenient. These services often provide a safe and reliable way to get around, especially late at night.

Staying connected with friends and family while traveling is important for safety. Share your itinerary and check in regularly. Consider using a travel app that allows you to share your location with trusted contacts. This way, someone always knows where you are and can assist if something goes wrong.

Navigating unfamiliar cities requires a balance of preparation and spontaneity. While planning is crucial, leaving room for unexpected discoveries can lead to some of themost memorable experiences. Allow yourself the freedom to wander off the beaten path and explore lesser-known areas. These adventures often reveal the true essence of a city, far from the typical tourist spots. However, always maintain a sense of situational awareness and avoid areas that are known to be unsafe.

Protecting Your Valuables

Traveling with valuable items can be a source of stress, but with the right precautions, you can significantly reduce the risk of loss or theft. Protecting your valuables starts before you even leave your home and continues throughout your journey. By taking a proactive approach, you can enjoy your travels with peace of mind, knowing that your possessions are secure.

Begin by carefully considering what you really need to bring. The fewer valuables you carry, the less you have to worry about. Items such as expensive jewelry or unnecessary electronics are best left at home. If you must bring high-value items, ensure they are covered by your travel insurance. Take photographs of these items and keep a detailed list, including serial numbers, to help with any potential claims.

Investing in quality luggage and accessories designed with security in mind is a smart move. Choose bags with sturdy zippers, lockable compartments, and slash-proof materials. Many modern travel bags feature built-in security features such as RFID-blocking pockets to protect against electronic pickpocketing. When packing, distribute valuables throughout your luggage to avoid having all your important items in one place.

While en route, keep your most important items—passport, wallet, phone, and any essential medications—in a carry-on bag that stays with you at all times. Use a crossbody bag or a money belt that can be worn under your clothes to keep these items close and secure. Avoid placing valuables in checked luggage, as it can be more susceptible to theft or mishandling.

Once you arrive at your destination, secure your valuables in a hotel safe or a locked drawer. Many hotels offer in-room safes, but if you have any doubts about their security, consider using a portable travel safe that can be secured to fixed objects. For added security, keep your room door locked at all times and use the additional latch or chain if available.

When out exploring, be mindful of how you carry your belongings. Use a bag that can be worn across your body with the strap diagonally, making it harder for thieves to snatch. Keep the bag in front of you and hold it close in crowded places. If you use a backpack, consider using a lock on the zippers and avoid keeping valuables in the outer compartments.

In public places, especially tourist hotspots, be extra vigilant. Pickpockets often target these areas, using distractions like street performances or crowded attractions to their advantage. Be cautious when approached by strangers asking for directions or trying to sell you something, as these can be tactics to divert your attention. Keeping your hands on your bag and staying aware of your surroundings can deter potential thieves.

Using technology wisely can also help protect your valuables. Enable tracking apps on your smartphone, tablet, or laptop. These apps can help you locate your devices if they are lost or stolen and can remotely lock or erase data to prevent unauthorized access. Additionally, back up important documents and photos to a secure cloud service, ensuring you have access to them even if your devices are compromised.

When dining out or visiting cafes, avoid placing your bag on the back of a chair or under the table where it's out of sight. Instead, keep it on your lap or use a bag hook to hang it from the table in front of you. This keeps your belongings within your line of vision and reduces the risk of someone taking advantage of an unattended bag.

Cash and cards require special attention. Carry only the amount of cash you need for the day and keep the rest in a secure location, such as your hotel safe. Spread your cards across different locations—carry one with you and keep a backup in a separate, secure place. This way, if you lose your wallet, you still have access to funds. Consider using travel credit cards that offer fraud protection and can be easily canceled and replaced if lost or stolen.

When using ATMs, choose machines located inside banks or well-lit areas, and be aware of your surroundings. Shield your PIN entry and avoid using ATMs that look tampered with or have any unusual attachments. If possible, limit your withdrawals to reduce the number of times you expose yourself to potential risks.

Another important aspect of protecting your valuables is understanding local scams and crime tactics. Research common scams in your destination before you go, so you can recognize and avoid them. For example, some places are notorious for distraction techniques, while others might have issues with fake taxi drivers or inflated prices in tourist areas.

Developing a few good habits can go a long way in protecting your valuables. Make it a routine to check that you have all your important items before leaving any location—whether it's a café, a museum, or a taxi. Being consistent with these checks helps ensure nothing is left behind or forgotten.

Sometimes, despite all precautions, things can still go wrong. Having a plan for such situations is crucial. Know the contact details of your country's embassy or consulate, and understand the process for reporting lost or stolen items. Keep copies of important documents, such as your passport and insurance policy, both digitally and physically in separate locations.

Traveling with confidence and security involves a mix of preparation, smarthabits, and awareness. By taking comprehensive measures to protect your valuables, you not

only safeguard your possessions but also enhance your overall
travel experience.

Ensuring your health and taking necessary medical precautions are paramount when traveling, especially to unfamiliar destinations. Proper planning and awareness can prevent many common health issues and ensure a smoother, more enjoyable journey. This chapter delves into essential steps to safeguard your well-being before, during, and after your trip.

Before embarking on any trip, it's crucial to research your destination's health risks and necessary vaccinations. The Centers for Disease Control and Prevention (CDC) and the World Health Organization (WHO) provide up-to-date information on required and recommended vaccines for different countries. Schedule a visit to a travel clinic or your healthcare provider at least six to eight weeks before departure. This allows ample time for vaccinations, which may require multiple doses or take time to become effective. Common vaccinations for travelers include those for hepatitis A and B, typhoid, yellow fever, and rabies.

In addition to vaccinations, ensure you have a supply of any prescription medications you might need, along with documentation from your doctor. Carry a copy of your prescriptions, including the generic names of the medications, as brand names can vary internationally. It's also wise to bring a letter from your healthcare provider explaining your medical conditions and the necessity of your medications, particularly if you are traveling with controlled substances.

Pack a well-stocked travel health kit to address common ailments and injuries. Include over-the-counter medications for pain and fever (like ibuprofen or acetaminophen), antihistamines for allergies, anti-diarrheal medications, rehydration salts, and a basic first aid kit with bandages, antiseptic wipes, and antibiotic ointment. Tailor your kit to your specific needs and the nature of your destination. For instance, if you're traveling to a region with a high risk of mosquito-borne diseases, include insect repellent containing DEET or picaridin, and consider packing a mosquito net.

Understanding the local healthcare system is vital. Research the location of the nearest hospitals or clinics, and know the emergency contact numbers for the area. If you have health insurance, verify whether it covers international travel. If not, consider purchasing travel insurance that includes medical coverage. This can provide peace of mind and financial protection in case of serious illness or injury abroad.

During your trip, maintaining good hygiene practices is one of the most effective ways to prevent illness. Wash your hands frequently with soap and water, especially before eating or after using the bathroom. Hand sanitizer with at least 60% alcohol is a good alternative when soap and water are not available. Be mindful of food and water safety, particularly in regions where waterborne diseases are common. Drink bottled or purified water, avoid ice cubes, and eat food that is thoroughly cooked. Raw fruits and vegetables should be washed with clean water or peeled.

Altitude sickness can be a concern when traveling to high-altitude destinations. Symptoms include headaches, nausea, dizziness, and fatigue. To mitigate these effects, ascend gradually to allow your body to acclimate, stay hydrated, and avoid alcohol and strenuous exercise in the first 24 hours. Over-the-counter medications like acetazolamide can also help prevent and treat altitude sickness, but consult your healthcare provider before use.

Heat-related illnesses, such as heat exhaustion and heat stroke, are risks in hot climates. Stay hydrated by drinking plenty of fluids, wear lightweight and loose-fitting clothing, and take breaks in shaded or air-conditioned areas. Be aware of the symptoms of heat exhaustion—such as heavy sweating, weakness, and dizziness—and act quickly to cool down if they occur.

Conversely, cold climates pose their own health risks, including hypothermia and frostbite. Dress in layers to retain body heat, wear a hat and gloves, and stay dry. Recognize the signs of hypothermia, such as shivering, confusion, and slurred speech, and seek immediate shelter and warmth if they arise.

Mosquito-borne diseases like malaria, dengue fever, and Zika virus can be significant concerns in tropical and subtropical regions. Use insect repellent, wear long sleeves and pants, and sleep under a mosquito net if necessary. For malaria prevention, take prescribed antimalarial medications before, during, and after your trip as directed by your healthcare provider.

Another critical aspect of travel health is understanding and respecting your body's limits. Jet lag, fatigue, and the physical demands of travel can take a toll. Try to get adequate rest before your trip, stay hydrated, and allow time to adjust to new time zones. Short naps, exposure to natural light, and staying active can help mitigate the effects of jet lag.

Mental health is as important as physical health. Traveling can be stressful, and it's essential to recognize signs of anxiety or depression. Take time to relax, engage in activities you enjoy, and stay connected with loved ones. If you have a history of mental health issues, continue any prescribed treatments and consider discussing your travel plans with a mental health professional.

Upon returning home, continue to monitor your health, especially if you've traveled to areas with prevalent infectious diseases. Some illnesses can have delayed onset symptoms. If you feel unwell, seek medical attention andinform your healthcare provider about your recent travel history. This information can be crucial for accurate diagnosis and timely treatment.

Emergency Preparation and Contacts

Traveling can be an exhilarating experience, but it also comes with its share of uncertainties. Preparing for emergencies and knowing who to contact can make a significant difference in how you handle unexpected situations. This chapter will guide you through essential steps to ensure you are well-prepared for any emergencies that may arise while traveling.

Before you embark on your journey, it's crucial to gather all necessary information about your destination. Research the local emergency services, including police, medical services, and fire departments. In many countries, the emergency number is not 911, so make sure you know the correct number to dial. Additionally, familiarize yourself with the location of the nearest embassy or consulate. These institutions can be invaluable resources if you lose your passport, get arrested, or face other serious issues.

Creating a comprehensive emergency contact list is a vital step. Include contact information for family members or friends back home, your country's embassy or consulate, local emergency services, and your travel insurance provider. Store this list in multiple places: a physical copy in your wallet, a digital copy on your phone, and perhaps even an email copy that you can access online. This redundancy ensures that you have access to this critical information even if one method fails.

Travel insurance is another essential aspect of emergency preparation. A good travel insurance policy can cover a wide range of emergencies, including medical issues, trip cancellations, lost luggage, and even evacuations. Read the fine print to understand what is covered and what is not. Some policies may require you to pay upfront and then seek reimbursement, so be prepared for this possibility. Always carry a copy of your insurance policy details and the contact information for your insurer.

Medical emergencies can be particularly daunting when you are far from home. Before you leave, consult with your healthcare provider about any necessary vaccinations and medications you may need. If you have a chronic condition, carry a sufficient supply of your medications, and bring a letter from your doctor detailing your condition and treatment. This letter can be crucial if you need medical assistance abroad.

Pack a basic first aid kit tailored to your needs. Include items such as adhesive bandages, antiseptic wipes, pain relievers, and any prescription medications you may need. If you are traveling to a remote area, consider adding a more comprehensive medical kit, including items like a splint, sterile syringes, and a suture kit. Knowing how to use these items is equally important, so consider taking a basic first aid course before your trip.

If you have any severe allergies, wear a medical alert bracelet and carry an epinephrine auto-injector. It's also a good idea to learn the local language for common emergency phrases, such as "I am allergic to peanuts" or "I need a doctor." This knowledge can be lifesaving in situations where communication is a barrier.

Natural disasters, such as earthquakes, hurricanes, and floods, can occur with little warning. Research the types of natural disasters that are common in your destination and understand the local protocols for dealing with them. For example, if you are traveling to a region prone to earthquakes, familiarize yourself with the safest places to take cover. If hurricanes are a risk, know the evacuation routes and the location of emergency shelters.

Civil unrest and political instability can also pose significant risks to travelers. Before you leave, check the travel advisories issued by your government. These advisories provide valuable information about the safety of your destination and can help you make informed decisions. If you find yourself in a situation of civil unrest, try to stay indoors and avoid large gatherings. Contact your embassy or consulate for advice and assistance.

Having a communication plan is essential in any emergency. Ensure your phone is unlocked so you can use a local SIM card if necessary. Alternatively, consider an international roaming plan that covers your destination. Apps like WhatsApp, Skype, and

Viber can be useful for staying in touch with loved ones and emergency contacts. If you are traveling to an area with limited cell service, consider renting a satellite phone.

Knowing how to navigate your surroundings in an emergency is critical. Carry a map of the area and mark the locations of important places such as your hotel, the nearest hospital, police station, and embassy. If you rely on digital maps, download offline versions so you can access them without an internet connection. Familiarize yourself with the local public transportation system and have a few taxi numbers saved in your phone.

Money can be a significant concern in emergencies. Always carry some local currency in small denominations for immediate expenses. Additionally, have a backup credit card stored separately from your main wallet. Inform your bank of your travel plans to avoid having your cards frozen for suspicious activity. In case of theft, knowing how to quickly contact your bank to cancel cards and arrange for replacements is crucial.

Personal safety should always be a top priority. Trust your instincts and be aware of your surroundings. Avoid risky areas, especially at night, and do not display valuables such as expensive jewelry or large amounts of cash. If you are confronted by a thief, it is usually safer to comply rather than resist. Your safety is more important thanyour belongings.

Chapter 4: Top Destinations for Solo Travelers

Solo travel can be one of the most enriching and liberating experiences. It allows you to explore the world on your own terms, make spontaneous decisions, and immerse yourself fully in new cultures without the need to compromise. However, choosing the right destination is crucial to ensure safety, accessibility, and a fulfilling experience. This chapter highlights some of the top destinations for solo travelers, offering a blend of adventure, culture, and safety.

Japan is a top contender for solo travelers. Known for its low crime rates and efficient public transportation, Japan offers a seamless travel experience. Tokyo's bustling metropolis provides an endless array of activities, from exploring high-tech districts like Shibuya and Akihabara to visiting serene temples and gardens. The Japanese culture of respect and politeness ensures that even if you don't speak the language, locals are often willing to help. Kyoto, with its historical temples and traditional tea houses, offers a tranquil contrast to Tokyo's fast pace. For nature enthusiasts, a visit to the Japanese Alps or the hot springs in Hakone provides a serene escape.

Moving westward, Iceland is another excellent destination for solo travelers. Renowned for its stunning landscapes and natural wonders, Iceland offers a sense of adventure and solitude. Reykjavik, the capital, is small and walkable, making it easy to navigate. The Icelandic people are known for their friendliness, and the country ranks high in global safety indices. Renting a car allows you to explore the dramatic scenery at your own pace, from the Golden Circle and its geysers and waterfalls to the otherworldly landscapes of the Snaefellsnes Peninsula. The Northern Lights, visible during the winter months, are a spectacular sight that shouldn't be missed.

New Zealand is a paradise for solo travelers seeking adventure and natural beauty. With its diverse landscapes, from the rolling hills of Hobbiton to the rugged peaks of the Southern Alps, New Zealand offers a wealth of outdoor activities. Queenstown, known as the adventure capital of the world, provides opportunities for bungee jumping, skydiving, and hiking. The country's excellent infrastructure and well-marked trails make it easy for solo hikers to explore safely. The Maori culture adds a rich layer of history and tradition, which can be experienced through cultural shows and visits to traditional villages.

In Europe, Portugal stands out as a top destination for solo travelers. Lisbon, the vibrant capital, is known for its colorfulneighborhoods, historic trams, and lively fado music. The city's compact size makes it easy to explore on foot or by public transport. Solo travelers can enjoy strolling through the narrow streets of Alfama, visiting the historic Belem Tower, or relaxing at one of the many rooftop bars. Porto, with its famous port wine cellars and picturesque riverside, offers a more laid-back vibe. The Algarve region, with its stunning beaches and charming coastal towns, is perfect for those looking to unwind.

Southeast Asia offers several destinations ideal for solo travelers, and Thailand is often at the top of the list. Known as the "Land of Smiles," Thailand's welcoming culture makes it easy for solo travelers to feel at home. Bangkok, with its bustling markets, grand palaces, and vibrant street life, provides an exciting urban experience. Chiang Mai, in the north, offers a more relaxed atmosphere with its temples, night markets, and opportunities for trekking in the nearby mountains. The islands in the south, such as Koh Phi Phi and Koh Samui, are perfect for beach lovers and offer a range of accommodations from budget hostels to luxury resorts.

Australia is another fantastic destination for solo travelers, offering a mix of cosmopolitan cities and vast natural landscapes. Sydney, with its iconic Opera House and Harbour Bridge, is a dynamic city with plenty to see and do. Melbourne, known for its artsy vibe, cafes, and street art, provides a different urban experience. The Great Barrier Reef is a must-visit for snorkeling and diving enthusiasts, while the Outback offers a chance to explore Australia's rugged interior. The country's excellent safety record and English-speaking population make it particularly accessible for solo travelers.

In South America, Colombia has emerged as a top destination for solo travelers, shedding its past reputation and becoming known for its vibrant culture and friendly locals. Bogota, the capital, offers a mix of modern and colonial architecture, while Medellin, once infamous, is now celebrated for its innovation and transformation. Cartagena, with its colorful streets and Caribbean beaches, provides a unique blend of history and relaxation. The coffee region, with its lush landscapes and charming fincas, is perfect for those looking to explore rural Colombia.

Finally, for those seeking a blend of history, culture, and modernity, Turkey is an excellent choice. Istanbul, straddling Europe and Asia, offers a rich tapestry of experiences. From the grandeur of the Hagia Sophia and the Blue Mosque to the bustling Grand Bazaar and the vibrant Istiklal Street, Istanbul is a city that never ceases to amaze. Cappadocia, with its unique rock formations and hot air balloon rides, provides a surreal landscape that is perfect for exploration. The coastaltowns along the Turkish Riviera, such as Antalya and Bodrum, offer beautiful beaches, clear waters, and ancient ruins, making them ideal for both relaxation and historical exploration.

Europe: The Best Cities for Solo Exploration

Europe offers a tapestry of diverse cultures, historical landmarks, and vibrant urban life, making it an ideal continent for solo exploration. Each city has its unique charm and atmosphere, ensuring that solo travelers can find a destination that fits their interests and preferences. From the romantic streets of Paris to the bustling markets of Istanbul, Europe's cities provide a rich array of experiences that cater to the solo adventurer.

Paris, often known as the City of Light, is a dream destination for many solo travelers. The city's iconic landmarks, such as the Eiffel Tower, Notre-Dame Cathedral, and the Louvre Museum, offer endless opportunities for exploration. Walking along the Seine River, you can admire the historic bridges and vibrant street life, stopping at quaint cafes for a croissant and coffee. The city's neighborhoods, each with its distinct character, are perfect for wandering. The artistic Montmartre, with its bohemian vibe, offers charming streets and panoramic views of the city from the Sacré-Cœur Basilica. Meanwhile, the Marais district is known for its trendy boutiques, galleries, and historic architecture. Paris's efficient metro system makes it easy to navigate, and the city's love for culture and art ensures that there is always something to see and do.

Barcelona, with its unique blend of modernism and tradition, is another fantastic city for solo travelers. The works of Antoni Gaudí, including the famous Sagrada Família and Park Güell, provide a surreal and captivating experience. The city's Gothic Quarter, with its narrow medieval streets, hidden squares, and historic buildings, invites exploration and discovery. Barcelona's vibrant beach scene, particularly at Barceloneta Beach, offers a perfect spot to relax and soak in the Mediterranean sun. The city's culinary scene, known for its tapas and seafood, is best enjoyed at the bustling markets such as La Boqueria. Barcelona's lively nightlife, with its numerous bars and clubs, ensures that solo travelers can easily meet new people and enjoy the city's energetic atmosphere.

Amsterdam, with its picturesque canals and laid-back vibe, is a city that feels welcoming to solo travelers. The city's compact size and excellent public transportation make it easy to get around. Biking is a popular mode of transport, and renting a bicycle allows you to explore the city like a local. The Anne Frank House, Van Gogh Museum, and Rijksmuseum offer deep dives into history and art. The Jordaanneighborhood, with its narrow streets, independent shops, and cozy cafes, is perfect for a leisurely day of wandering. Amsterdam's coffee shops and vibrant nightlife provide ample opportunities for socializing and meeting fellow travelers. The city's relaxed and open-minded atmosphere ensures that solo travelers feel at ease.

Prague, with its fairy-tale charm and rich history, is a city that captivates solo travelers. The city's well-preserved medieval architecture, including the iconic Charles Bridge and Prague

Castle, offers a journey back in time. Strolling through the Old Town Square, you can admire the Astronomical Clock and the stunning Gothic and Baroque buildings. The city's numerous gardens and parks, such as Letná Park, provide peaceful retreats with beautiful views of the city. Prague's thriving arts scene, with its numerous theaters, galleries, and music venues, ensures that there is always something cultural to experience. The city's affordable prices and friendly locals make it an attractive destination for solo travelers on a budget.

Vienna, with its imperial grandeur and cultural richness, is a city that offers a sophisticated solo travel experience. The city's stunning palaces, such as Schönbrunn and the Hofburg, provide a glimpse into its royal past. Vienna's coffee house culture, with its elegant cafes and delicious pastries, invites you to relax and soak in the city's ambiance. The Ringstrasse, a grand boulevard encircling the city center, is lined with impressive buildings, including the State Opera House and the Parliament. Vienna's music heritage, associated with composers like Mozart and Beethoven, can be experienced through concerts and performances at various venues. The city's efficient public transportation system and safe environment make it easy for solo travelers to explore.

Lisbon, with its sunny weather and vibrant neighborhoods, is a city that feels warm and inviting. The city's historic tram 28 offers a scenic ride through its narrow streets and hills, providing beautiful views of the city and the Tagus River. The Alfama district, with its maze-like streets and traditional Fado music, offers a glimpse into Lisbon's soul. The city's numerous viewpoints, such as Miradouro da Senhora do Monte, provide breathtaking panoramas. Lisbon's culinary scene, known for its seafood and pastries, is best experienced at the local markets and traditional restaurants. The city's friendly locals and relaxed pace make it an ideal destination for solo travelers looking to unwind.

Berlin, known for its dynamic history and contemporary culture, is a city that offers a diverse solo travel experience. The city's landmarks, such as the Berlin Wall, Brandenburg Gate, and the Reichstag, provide insights into its complex past. Berlin's numerous museums, including the Museum Island and the Berlin History Museum, offer a deep dive into art and history. The city's neighborhoods,such as Kreuzberg and Neukölln, are known for their vibrant street art, eclectic cafes, and multicultural atmosphere. These areas provide a glimpse into Berlin's creative and alternative scene. The extensive public transportation network and the city's bike-friendly infrastructure make it easy to navigate and explore.

Asia: Exotic and Welcoming Destinations

Asia, a continent of contrasts and diversity, presents solo travelers with a multitude of exotic and welcoming destinations. From bustling metropolises to serene landscapes, Asia offers rich cultural experiences, ancient traditions, and vibrant modernity. Each destination provides a unique blend of history, culture, and natural beauty that captivates and comforts solo adventurers.

Thailand stands out as one of Asia's most popular destinations for solo travelers. Known as the "Land of Smiles," Thailand's friendly locals and tourist infrastructure make it exceptionally welcoming. Bangkok, the capital, is a city of contrasts where modern skyscrapers tower over golden temples. The Grand Palace, Wat Arun, and Wat Pho, home to the famous reclining Buddha, offer glimpses into Thailand's rich heritage. The city's street food scene is legendary, with markets like Chatuchak and the numerous night markets offering delicious and affordable culinary delights. For a quieter pace, Chiang Mai in the north offers a more relaxed atmosphere with its ancient temples, lush mountains, and vibrant cultural festivals. The islands of the south, such as Phuket and Koh Samui, provide idyllic beaches and a laid-back vibe, perfect for sunbathing, snorkeling, and island hopping.

Japan, with its blend of ancient tradition and cutting-edge modernity, is another captivating destination for solo travelers. Tokyo, the sprawling capital, dazzles with its neon-lit districts, towering skyscrapers, and bustling streets. Yet, amidst the urban hustle, serene temples and traditional gardens offer peaceful retreats. The historic city of Kyoto, with its stunning temples, shrines, and geisha districts, provides a deep dive into Japan's cultural heritage. Kyoto's Arashiyama Bamboo Grove and Fushimi Inari Shrine are must-visit spots that exude tranquility and spiritual significance. Japan's efficient public transportation system, particularly the Shinkansen or bullet trains, makes traveling between cities seamless. The country's respect for personal space and safety makes it an ideal destination for solo explorers.

Vietnam, with its breathtaking landscapes and rich history, offers a diverse range of experiences for solo travelers. Hanoi, the capital, is a city where ancient traditions blend with French colonial architecture. The Old Quarter, with its narrow streets and bustling markets, is perfect for wandering and discovering local life. The city's many lakes, such as HoanKiem Lake, provide serene spots for reflection amidst the urban chaos. Ho Chi Minh City, in the south, pulsates with energy and offers insights into Vietnam's modern history through sites like the War Remnants Museum and the Cu Chi Tunnels. For natural beauty, Halong Bay's towering limestone islands and emerald waters provide a stunning backdrop for cruises and kayaking. The ancient town of Hoi An, with its lantern-lit streets and preserved architecture, offers a charming and picturesque escape.

Indonesia's Bali is a paradise for solo travelers seeking both adventure and tranquility. Known for its lush landscapes, vibrant culture, and spiritual retreats, Bali offers a rich tapestry of experiences. Ubud, the cultural heart of the island, is renowned for its traditional arts, yoga retreats, and the Sacred Monkey Forest Sanctuary. The town's rice terraces, particularly those in Tegallalang, provide breathtaking scenery and opportunities for peaceful walks. Bali's beaches, such as those in Seminyak and Uluwatu, offer excellent surfing, sunbathing, and vibrant nightlife. For a more secluded experience, the island of Nusa Penida, with its dramatic cliffs and crystal-clear waters, is perfect for diving, snorkeling, and exploring hidden beaches.

India, with its diverse cultures, historic landmarks, and vibrant cities, is a destination that promises unforgettable experiences for solo travelers. Delhi, the bustling capital, is a city of contrasts where ancient monuments like the Red Fort and Qutub Minar stand alongside modern developments. The city's markets, such as Chandni Chowk, offer a sensory overload of sights, sounds, and flavors. Jaipur, part of India's Golden Triangle, enchants with its pink-hued architecture, majestic palaces, and vibrant bazaars. The iconic Taj Mahal in Agra, a symbol of love and architectural brilliance, is a must-visit. For a spiritual journey, Varanasi, one of the world's oldest cities, offers a profound experience with its ghats along the Ganges River and daily rituals. India's extensive rail network makes traveling between cities accessible and offers a glimpse into the country's diverse landscapes and cultures.

South Korea, with its mix of ancient traditions and modern innovations, offers a dynamic experience for solo travelers. Seoul, the vibrant capital, is a city where skyscrapers and palaces coexist. The Gyeongbokgung Palace and BukchonHanok Village provide insights into Korea's royal history and traditional architecture. The city's bustling districts, such as Myeongdong and Hongdae, are known for shopping, street food, and nightlife. For natural beauty, Jeju Island, often referred to as the "Hawaii of Korea," offers stunning beaches, volcanic landscapes, and scenic hiking trails. South Korea's efficient public transportation and high level of safety make it anexcellent destination for solo travelers. The country's widespread use of technology, from high-speed internet to digital maps, ensures that navigating and exploring is straightforward and convenient.